Just for the Record

Nance Cookson

Just for the Record

Collected Poems

GP

Just for the Record: Collected Poems
ISBN 978 1 76041 481 8

First published separately as *All the Time Left* 1999,
Laughing in the Street 2006 and *The Question, the Answer* 2009

This collected edition published 2018 by
GINNINDERRA PRESS
PO Box 3461 Port Adelaide SA 5015
www.ginninderrapress.com.au

Contents

All the Time Left

Recall

It's funny how the memory
grabs you suddenly – like the
dropping of a hand
upon your shoulder.

Association of ideas
can cause the spark
and times long past
and hidden
in the cavities of the brain
are there again.

You hear the
laughter,
the joy of
each December.

And, when the days
are cold and long,
it's good to have
the laughter
to remember.

Different Then

I was young once;
it was different
then.

Sometimes, when I
read the papers
I wish that I was
young again,
but only
on good
news days.

I Can Remember

I can remember,
when the introduction
of a malted milk,
was as important

to me
as the landing
on the moon
was to my grandchildren.

Comparisons, it's said,
are odious,
well,
maybe so.

But life
wasn't odious then.
Or, if it was,
I didn't know it.

Old Age

'It was different then,'
she said, her voice in a whisper.
(I sat there taking notes.)
'But the past's always better,
All generations
will tell you that.'

(She still had that
twinkle in her eye.)
'Progress isn't all bad.'
(Tease – she wouldn't elaborate.)
'The postman always
blew a whistle –
I miss that.
No one writes today, though,
so what does it matter?'
She wiped a tear,
and so did I.

Slow Pace

I like
the slow
pace
of life.

I don't think
snails
have heart attacks.

An argument
should unfold
as gently
as the
blooming of a rose.

And all
agreements
should be
cemented
in the strength
of a well-meant
handshake.

Patience

The old man
in the nursing home
sat working out the puzzle.
Gnarled, arthritic
hands pushed the
pieces into place.
Intrigued
by his patience
I sat silently by.
'You didn't give him
much company,'
said a visitor passing by.
I reeled at his insensitivity.
'He's old – not deaf,' I said
to myself.
When the puzzle
was miraculously and
patiently completed
the old man winked (deliciously)
at me.
'Hope you'll come next week,'
he said.
'Some of them drive you mad
with their chatter.'

Levels of Patience

I waited for the sun
to rise,
you waited for the
fish to bite.

We exercised patience
at different
levels.

My certainty
was there
before me.

Your chances
could amount
to nil.

My sun
could be
over the
yardarm.
You could
be fishing
still!

Listening To a Saying

'You're telling me,'
He'd say,
My American
grandfather.
It was his way
of talking,
a sort of phrase
he'd use.
I haven't heard anyone
say it for years.
Sayings die but revival
is around the corner.
'That's a big fish
you've caught,'
I say to the boy
on the pier.
'You're telling me,' he replies.
'Do you have an American grandfather?'
I ask him.
'Nah,' he says and goes on fishing;
laughs a bit at an old lady.

Bonza

Now, there's a word
from yesterday.
Moved aside,
just died,
gone, like the lemmings.

I missed the funeral,
the wake,
the ritual.

Bonza: purely Australian,
no naturalisation ceremony
needed.

What's taken its place?
'Great' I suppose
or
'triffic'.
Yes 'triffic',
that's the word,
but 'great's more upper-crust.

'Bonza' never was (upper-crust),
that was part of the fun of it.
'Real beaut and bobby dazzler',
'bonza' said it all.

Pocket Dictionaries

They don't make pockets
big enough
for dictionaries
these days.

I thought about it.
'Pocket Dictionary'
it said on the cover.

'They've put too many
words in it, that's why,'
said Mr Riley,
who usually spoke about
ten words a fortnight.

The Isms

There's: existentialism,
socialism,
communism,
atheism,
naturalism,
federalism,
individualism,
dogmatism,
heroism,
rheumatism,
sensationalism,
jingoism,
wowserism,
even tourism,
and, out of all
these,
I get botulism;
talk about pessimism.

Cloning

Cloning:
add a consonant
and you have *clowning*.
Observe: one small letter
making a difference
to a word
to a meaning.
But isn't cloning
clowning?
Think of a number,
double it;
think of a human;
ditto.
What will be
thought of next?
Take from the
dictionary
the word
'individuality'
('dignity' too
while you are at it).
Think of a person,
clone them.
Rubber-stamped
people.
It's enough
to turn you
back to religion.

I Heard About It

I heard about it
but the ears can deceive.
I spoke of it,
There was
disbelief.
'I'd check the papers
again on that one,'
said a fellow traveller,
Science and the study
of it
is a wonderful thing,
but the cloning of a bee
defies logic
no matter which way
you look at it.
Priorities are
important here
and
there's the sting!

A Place

We dream
Of a place
Those of us
Who need to dream
Design one
According to
Our needs
And imagination
Add colours
Set the scene
Then settle
When times are
Ready
Into this
Very necessary
Dream.

Coastal Shores

I'll walk
the coastal shores
one day;
study shells
and sea birds;
wonder,
when storms prevail,
at debris washed
upon the beach;
feel soft
and moving
sands beneath
my feet;
share, with a
cloudless sky,
the gentle sun
upon my back;
then let the blue-green
salty waves
cleanse and refresh me,
proving, beyond a doubt:
the most expensive
things are not
necessarily the best.

At Charlotte Pass

I see
the distant
snow-filled
silent clouds
that hang,
like pictures
on a
pale blue wall.
No movement yet,
but light and shade
are playing tricks
and the sun's rays
have made an appearance.

Slowly now,
they drift
and fade
slowly – slowly.
The hikers
will return
from breathless
tracks
pink-cheeked
and eager
to disclose
the beauty
they have
witnessed.

Journey

We took the hire car
to Silverton
(out of Broken Hill).
Or, to be more precise,
the car took us.
Four on the floor
and we're used to
the automatic
and the road is a bit like the
scenic railway in
sections.
It's dusty and rough,
but interesting.
Silverton – an almost
ghost town
full of history.
And, more than anything,
the colour of the place
takes you by surprise.
Its colour planned
for artists.

The Outback – Queensland To Darwin

'Free beer tomorrow.'
We laughed –
that is,
after the penny dropped.
Humour is like that in the
outback.

The long straight
road to Darwin
is full of surprises.
Flat plains
domed by blue
and never-ending
cloudless skies;
kites and eagles
soaring.

'Fresh kangaroos today,
fellows,'
they may well
squawk
as food presents itself
off macadamised road plates.
Yes, 'Free beer tomorrow,'
that's what the sign on the
pub window said. Took
a minute before the joke sank in.

Spring Has Come Now

And spring has come now.
The sun-drenched earth
is cracking
like stale honeycomb.

Winter,
you have bypassed us.
The cattle feed or strive to feed,
on grass,
long burnt
and farmers,
their strength in unity,
survey the scene
and dream
of other times.

October Night

We dined Chinese,
our three bearded men
in attendance.

The poetry launch a great
success we moved on;
conversation and laughter
flowed freely.

Exchanged ideas,
philosophised a bit,
one glass of wine enough
to warm the spirit and the soul.

Afterwards – outside the pub
and a noisy farewell.
'Time to move on,'
laughed John.
'We could be arrested for this.'

The late October night was
cool; more like September.
Warm now, and in the car
it's the laughter I remember.

Uninvited

Uninvited
they came
and, uninvited,
stayed.

The heat of
the day
had something
to do
with the
irritability
of it all.
They had a
better time
than we
did;
ruled the
roost actually.

'A sign of rain coming,'
Grandpa said.
'Brings ants to a picnic
every time.'

Observance

Before dusk
the day's toil
almost done
I seek a vantage point
to sit and watch
the setting of the sun.

Then, after nightfall
when the stars are
at their peak
I wonder at the moon
and drift
contentedly to sleep.

Bird calls come,
the early morning mists
have not quite risen.
I wait for sunrise
to learn
there is no greater vision.

A Daylight Robbery

Blue skies,
bright sunshine,
warm, soft breezes
blowing.

No indication of how
the day would evolve.

The obscenity of robbery
makes imprints on the
mind.

It's like watching a
freak show.

Desperate faces to
run with well-worn sneakers.

A stolen car, noisy
exhaust, the screeching
of car tyres. Shock tactics
that hang in the air.

The audience looks on
in disgust;
robbery is not a pleasant thing
to observe.
The obscenity of it makes imprints
on the mind.

Afterwards

It was afterwards
that words came.
Action on my part
was slow.

Eye contact was
the most
memorable thing.

There was a coldness
on the wharf
when our eyes met.
Icy winds
blew fast
and strong.

I wondered
all about it
later.
You had not been
there very long.

'What now,'
your eyes said
in desperation.

I stood
in panic
and in fear

There was little
time for
contemplation
and, far too late,
there came my tear.

I wanted to help.
I knew that
something
must be done.

I saw you flounder
on the wharf,
such a lonely
desperate one.

Too late
to fling
you in the
water.

Your only chance
and I had failed.
I could have saved
your life.

Dear fish,
I should be jailed.

Your desperate
eyes
still haunt me.
As I recall,
I looked away.
You had little time to
judge me
on the wharf
on that cold day.

I'd like to say
I'm sorry, fish,
and lay the blame
elsewhere;
on the fisherman
who caught you
and left you lying there.

But it's still
your eyes
that haunt me
as they pleaded
all in vain
as the cold winds
blew around me
as I stood there
in the rain.

From the National Library To the Memory of the Fallen

From the National Library
I watch the eastern wind
blow Japanese maples,
and glimpse across the lake
to behold, between movement,
the war memorial.
   Willow trees throw shadows
near water's edge
and distant, moving cars
distract me.
   There is warmth
in the library;
outside, showers send
the people running.
   No longer
do you have the need
to run
but we,
who read, and know
your history,
will remember you.

That Golden Opportunity

We missed that golden
opportunity
you and I.
Who knows
how life would have
shaped our destiny?
Dreams differ
from realities.

And the dream
held in abeyance
can at least be
enjoyed in escapism.

Laughing in the Street

Laughing in the Street

I awake to the sound
Of children
Laughing in
The street

To the warmth
Of sunshine
The song
Of the butcher-bird

Then I awake to the
Ever-lasting revelation
That all these things
Mean nothing
To those
In a war zone.

Between sleep
And waking
It all
Turns sour.

From Harrietville To Omeo

Surrounded in cloud
The road too narrow now
To turn back
The windscreen wipers
Working overtime
To no effect

We hold our breath
Or, in Delia's case
We shout our lungs out
Go slow, stop,
Ohmygod she screams
At repetitive intervals

There used to be views
From here once
She says
At some stage.

The snow poles guide us
When we can see them
And the danger signs
Seem to be inches apart

I won't come this way again
On and on she goes.

You've got that right
Says Joe
His hands clasped tightly
On the wheel

I catch sight of his face
In the mirror
He is pale
With exhaustion

Afterwards when we emerge
Into a weak and flimsy sunshine
At Omeo
We leave the car
For coffee and cake
And Joe takes my arm

No wonder men leave home to
Join the Foreign Legion
He smiles

Not caring whether
She hears him or not.

Tasmania

I'm down under
Down under
Deep waters divide me
From upper cities

(Or so it seems)

No chain connects me
To mainlands

(Now there's
A thought)

If some say
Convicts made me
I say
They did well.

The Gordon River

We hold our breath
To speak in hushed whispers

This place
Commands respect

Who would
Contemplate change?

Our warm heart beats
The cold clear air
Presents to us
Its alien features

Tasmania
A place apart.

At Jindabyne

It's ten degrees Celsius
At Jindabyne
And we're dreaming
Of north Queensland

'You can't smell
Sugar cane
At Jindabyne'
Says Joe

(In the year's
Understatement)
'Or tickle your toes
In the surf'

After winter
We'll paint the
Lounge room walls
Get rid of all the
Smudge and smear
That open fires cause

'Or move back to
The Sunshine Coast'
Says Joe again
With tunnel-vision
Philosophy.

You Were There

On the corner of
Nothing-much-going-on Street
A thousand or more years ago now
You were there

I remember

You were there
When guardian angels
Were ten a penny
And when there was
No great need for them

Now, when there is
Great need
Where are
They?

You

You walked out on
That algebra class
Slammed your book
On the desk

Wore pride on your sleeve
At poor exam results
And sailed
To war

In the aftermath of it all
War was more difficult
To understand than algebra
And not as easy
To walk away from

Even though
The desperation
To do so
Was ever present.

Of Love and Laughter

I will tell you stories of love
My little man
Of laughter;
Stories of faith and of belief

We will converse
On the wonder of the Earth
The pattern of the stars
The brightness
And the lightness
Of the moon

We will walk through valleys
Drink from pure clean streams
Listen to the birds of song
And one day listen
As the crickets chirp

We will make the most of it
We will not talk at all of war
For that will come
Soon enough

And we won't talk
Of shattered faith
Or disbelief
Or man's inhumanity to man

Under thick and heavy carpets
I will sweep these thing from you

Until the act of war resurfaces
And makes of me a schemer.

Mitche's Jetty

We swam at Mitche's Jetty
Most of the summer months
Took in the salt-sea air
Blue skies and soft sea breezes

Photographed fishing boats
Chugging into shore, pelicans following
And vowed to return
When winter had taken its holiday

But the act of war got in the way
And I saw your soldier's life as ordered
So, as it is often said
Things were 'put on hold'

The temporary sound of that
Shifted into permanency
And when soldiers stay away too long
The waiting game begins

When the act of war got in the way
Once more
I saw your soldier's life
As ordered.

The soft sea breezes
Still blow in near Mitche's Jetty
The blue clear water
Ripples still on shore

And the fishing boats
Still harbour with their
Catch again,
Much as before

Memories now are all I have
Of Mitche's Jetty
Swimming as we did
Those summer months

But soldiers stay away
Sometimes forever
The act of war
Will steal them from your side

And in my mind
I see us back at Mitche's Jetty
Swimming into shore
This time against the tide.

Humble Pie

We ate Humble Pie
At Billie Nudgell
Hungry as hunters
Home from the woods

Thought about the swims
At Alexandra Headland
Wished the sands
Still invaded our toes

The only thing we got
Really fed up with
Was all the traffic
Clogging the lanes

We could never get
Enough of
Humble Pie
At Billie Nudgell.

Theorists

Flat-earth policy
Theorists
Stand firm
In their belief

Everyone's opinion
Is important
And who would live
In a world where
Freedom of thought
And democracy
Are extinct

Don't we love
To thrive on characters
The more the merrier
I would say

You could fall off the earth
Laughing.

Like a Capuchin Monk

We sit around the campfire
Talking till near sunrise

On his way to sleep
Joe douses the fire
While Billy Blake
The silent one, ambles by
And, like a Capuchin monk
About to break his silence
Mumbles
From the corner of his mouth

'If ever they clone
The Invisible Man
Who
Would
Know?'

Wild Card

She's a rough one
She's a tough one
She's the farmer's
Wife

She's a strong one
A caring one
She's the farmer's
Life

She tends the sheep
And goats
With pleasure
And concern

Her weather-eye
Leaves little space
For trouble

She's the
Top of the crop
The farmer's wife
The farmer's life

She's a wild card

And, as for
The drover's wife
See 'Drysdale'
For reference and vision.

And Horses' Hooves

She still hears the sound of
Of horses' hooves
Her vision is
Of the trooper
And her fear
Is of the gun

She sees tears
In her mother's eyes
But no more
She sees her mother

Through the bleakness
Of time
She searches
For her
Siblings
And she feels shame

And she cannot
Understand it
For the shame
Is not hers
She knows
No explanation
For none is given

She is like
An answerless question
And there's no prize
To win
No prize to lose either
There's no prize

And the horses' hooves
Still echo in her ears
And her mother's tears
She sees
In every fall of rain.

Discovery

Visiting
Stratford on Avon
One day
Shakespeare was on
So I took
In a play

Later
I sat under
A tree nice
And shady
Thinking
Shakespeare
Married
An Avon lady.

Selling

We sold the cattle;
Drought conditions
Brought
Enforcement.

Myrna locked herself
In her room
And cried
For a week.

Then the rains came.
We should've waited
She
Said.

When floods prevailed
The soil soaked
Vegetable growth took on
The dying swan act

After that
Her sombre mood
Resigned itself
To the inevitability
Of the
Farmer's destiny.

Wild Things 1

I was the witness
If needed
To tell of the havoc
You caused

I was there
To relate
On the specified date
What you did to the coastal shores

You came in
With a roll call of thunder
Tore into the trees
Without pause

Such a wind like
I never had seen before
You lifted strong roofs
Broke down front and back doors

Wild events
Such as these
Are not meant
To please

But when
Nature
Decrees
There'll be more.

Nothing

There's nothing
As uninhibited
As crazy
Weather

It will take you
By surprise
Year after
Year

And nothing
Can control it
Nothing
Once it's
Hopelessly
Out of gear.

The Hero's Love

She had lived
To know
The scent
Of summer roses

She had lived
To feel
The gift of
Summer rain

And she'd learnt
For some short time
To love another

Until she sadly,
Wrongfully thought
He hadn't felt
The same

The one she loved
As we all knew
Was
Troubled

He was swimming
In a current
Of
Despair

He had no time
For romance
At that moment
He was desperate
He had a strong
Suspicion
There was
Murder in the air

Confusion in the matter
Was served upon a platter
Wrong moves were made
And panic was in play

And also
There were lots of
'Ifs' and 'onlys'
In the way
Then love's arrow
Fell to earth
And failed to blend
With the hearts
Of those who loved
And those he knew
He must defend

Revenge was strongly
Now on the agenda
The hero must act slowly
To succeed

He had learned the
Feel of hatred
In his body
He had learned how
Sad it was
A heart could bleed

Long and narrow
Ran the river
Silent
Strong

She had
No idea
He strove
To right a wrong

So without her sad
Goodbyes
She loosened
All the ties
Leaving Hamlet
To mournfully
Sing her song.

Ron Loves Betty

'Ron loves Betty'
Carved upon the tree
Forest fire gallops through
And the words
Are history.

Cucumber Sandwiches (Thinly Sliced)

Eating cucumber sandwiches
Thinly sliced
The tea
Poured into china cups
Delicate to the eye
Sipped with great gentility

Shaded by the ancient willow
We, in soft toned voices
And dressed in organdie frocks
Narrow velvet ribbons adorning,
Talk of other times

It is our annual Jane Austen day.
Transported in time we discuss her works
Talk of ironies and nuances
Remind ourselves that progress
Hasn't cancelled out the
Past entirely.

The Journey

We are on the freeway
Heading for the heart of town
Experiencing no joy at all
In this endeavour

Small cars are
Duelling with the semis
And petrol fumes
Fill our nostrils
With carcinogenic intent

If ever we were
Of high human intellect
Dispel this theory
Now

At overpasses
Road signs tell us
Far too late to notice
Which route is our best one

Inside the car
Fuming tempers rise
Sweet old grandmothers
Turn feral
And mother-in-law jokes
Aren't funny any more.

Raylene has forgotten
To bring the wedding present
So Troy shouts at her
Like a shark warning

There is no chance
In this frantic maze
Of turning back
So, for seemingly hours of
Expletive deleteds
We endure what our fates
Have decreed.

'Your driving hasn't improved'
Says Grandma
In a feeble attempt
To tone things down

'Nasty' says Troy
And Raylene starts crying.

'Get a life'
Says Grandma, going all modern
And the poisonous fumes
Within the car
Are worse than those outside

At the wedding
Someone says
'You all look well
You should drive down
More often'

And Australian humour
Rises to the occasion
But only for one
Brief moment

We have to drive
Home yet.   Get real!

As it's said in the Classics.

Eating Doughnuts

We are eating doughnuts
Jam thick
And sugar-crusted

Sipping lattes
At the Boardwalk
Café

'You'll be sorry,'
Coughs the thin
Gaunt miserable one

Puffing on fags
Lighting the next
As she stubs out the last.

Out of the Barrel

I dip my hand
Into a barrel-load of sayings
I come out with
'Grin and bear it'

Come on
Get real

Second dip
I come up with
'Stand up
And fight'

That's more like it

But jobs aren't ten
A penny any more and
There's mortgages
To deal with
Doctor's bills
To pay

Back to the barrel then
'Have a nice day.'

The Question, the Answer

The Shark

I'm walking away from Dobson's Point
They hauled in a large shark near the
Pier yesterday
Just where I'd seen the young boys
Taking long jumps, screaming with delight
Totally unaware of any danger

I'd thought about warning them
Someone had earlier but it
Only made their jumps
And leaps more eager

One day, they will talk about it,
One day, when grey hair, arthritic knees
And memory will allow them
It is most likely then that they will say
We must've been crazy.
Someone should have warned us.

Sardines

I'm eating a sardine sandwich
On a canvas seat
Near the pier

It's a sunny autumn
Afternoon
And nobody else is here

I look deep down
In the water
As the fish swim by

You would need
A hundred dozen fish
To bake a sardine pie

I hope that they don't
See me
Munching away at their kin

I feel a bit uncomfortable
As though
I've committed a sin

The sardine
Is a tiny fish
Relatively thin

He'd have to be
Of course you know
To fit inside a sardine tin.

Crayfish In the Pot

Boiling boiling
Slowly boiling
Crayfish
In the pot

Much larger
Than the yabbies
Although of them
There are a lot

Boiling boiling
Slowly let
Them
Simmer

I hear we have
Some VIPs
Coming here
For dinner

Boiling boiling
Never mind the pain
The reason for this dinner
I feel I must explain

It's about this
Annual event we hold
The winner gets
A bar of gold

Humanitarian awards
Are rare
Too bad poor crayfish
You are there

Boiling, boiling
Boiling in the pot.

Thinking About It

We have the ingredients here
People, money, time, themes,
Ideas, the theorists
Even the ratbags
Must have the ratbags to
Make the world go round

On camping trips
Your night time read
Was Hemingway
My choice always Steinbeck
Henry James close second
(loved *Washington Square*)

In matters music
Your love was of the Blues
While I was into other rythms
(love that sax, I melt like wax)
But when Artie Shaw played 'Frenisi'
That's when you agreed with me.

The Blarney Stone

It is said that you kissed
The blarney stone
I could believe that's true
A bit of blarney out of Killarney
Certainly isn't new

The Irish have a
Canny knack
Of making a dream come true
I don't suppose for a dollar or two
I could buy a Blarney stone
From you

You don't have to
Answer straight away
You can give it a bit of thought
But wouldn't I be the envied one
When everyone found out
What I bought?

Arguing

Get to the end of it
He says
You take too long

Some like the journey
On the way
The titbits, the incidentals

Not him,
Not that I'm reading him
The lesson mind you
Heaven forbid
And not that I'm bringing
Heaven into it either

He's an Atheist
(do you spell that with a capital letter?)
Not Pygmalion likely I would say

He denies it
'Agnostic' he says
Little difference, if you ask me.

The argument could go on forever
If I don't walk out the door
Or put on those ear muffs.

Spray Can Gran

Mervyn's grandma does graffiti
Mervyn's grandma what a hoot
You'd never think she had it in her
She's small and bent and rather cute

Mervyn's grandma got arrested
Caught red-handed near the bridge
Scrawling slogans with a spray can
Like a kid that's on the edge

Old age didn't stop the sentence
In the court the judge was stern
You, he said, *you're no example*
To the young on how to learn

His attitude was regimental
He treated grandma to a sneer
That was anything but sentimental
Get this vandal out of here

Mervyn's grandma's doing time
She believes that war's obscene
She says that everyone's entitled
To fulfil at least one dream

Sending youth to far-off battle
Long before their dreams ignite
Is a dangerous occupation
Grandma's fighting for their rights

NO MORE WAR PLEASE
Is her message emblazoned way up there in red
But it won't be seen by Mervyn
His war is over – he is dead.

Pairs

Two for the price of one
Is that not greed?
It seems today that more
Than one is what we need.

You must buy more.
Articles in stores
Are always
Packed in fours.

And when in doors
The fridge must house a feast
Three jars of this
Or two, the very least.

A cotton shirt
The same in green and white
One to wear each morning
The other for a summer night.

Why need two?
It's double Dutch to me.
Sometimes if you buy two
You get another free !

Extras. The Mormons often take
Another wife.
It works for them it seems.
That is their way of life.

It must be quite expensive though
At certain times,
Like special birthday celebrations,
Christmas, Easter time
and paying parking
fines.

Me, I'm grateful for
One pair of eyes,
To set things right
A bedside lamp to read
At night
An apple from the tree
To chew and bite
Maybe a pear or two
If that's all right.
And so it goes.
We deal in ones
And twos

Make that a double
Says the boozer
At the bar
And he's in trouble.

That Degas Painting

It's yours, Ducks,
She said

Your favourite painting;
Mine too; only a print of course
And the framing excellent
Look good on any wall.

Sheer good luck I won it
But you could feel the pain
The atmosphere electric
I kept my cool

Some on the committee
Thought I'd hand
It back
Fat chance.

Well now, it's yours, Ducks,
I've signed the proper papers
It's just a matter of time
Yes, it's yours.

I suppose there are some
Who will say
At the finish
Wicked old witch.

They will be wrong
You worked harder than most
You appreciated the work
For what it was

Wicked old witch
I hope that you
Laugh
When they say it.

Make sure
you get it when I go

I'd give it to you now
But those hungry wolves
Their eyes gleaming
All want a big piece of the pie

The largest slice of the cherry
I won't say ghouls
But what else is there
And what does it matter anyway

When my time comes
I'll take that smile on my face
Imagining their angst
when you get the Degas.

Wicked old witch
someone will say at the finish.

Standing In a Queue

You will find
Some don't mind
Standing in a queue

Others will go crazy
They will moan
And they will curse

Especially
In the winter time
When the rain comes
It is worse.

What is it that they queue for
It doesn't really matter
Some people I find gather there
Simply for a chatter.

The Old Town

We visit our old town
Hardly recognisable
No left turning where Casey's
Road once ran

We go in circles at the roundabout
And one-way streets
Puzzle us
Maze-like

But hard to take
Are the high-rise
That dominate
And cast their shadow.

And missing
Are the happy faces
That roamed the streets
Before the world moved on

Once More At Mitche's Jetty

Looking into the blue clear water
We watch the stingrays
Slide like glider clips on paper
Into their own environment

Flat as pancakes
Those out-of-space lookalikes
If your imagination takes you
That distance.

Beach Days

We were the young ones
The sun shone brighter on
The Portsea shores

Blond-headed boys
In the fire of youth
Drove their parents' cars

We watched them surf
In dangerous waters
None of us fearing consequences

Sunburnt and careless
We danced late into the night
Until the war came

And the blond-headed boys drove tanks
And surfed in more dangerous waters
And we learned to fear consequences

And the world changed

Fireside

We sit around the camp fire
Throwing in chestnuts
Reading poetry
Lots of Paterson (Banjo)
The Australian voice
Does him proud

Joe Tobias meant to bring
His C.J. Dennis edition
But being Joe
Forgot

Terry Warring helps out
Knows Dennis by rote
Recites snippets from
The Sentimental Bloke

We applaud

Someone reads Owen (Wilfred)
I'm not in the mood
For words of war
Although Owen
Does them best

'Move him into the sun'

Tears smart my eyes
A sudden wind
blows fierce

'Douse that fire'

We throw in stones and
Empty the thermos flasks
Harry's gran throws
Lemon slices that
Garnished the sardine
Platter, dead centre.
Good shot, Gran

Then the rain uninvited but
Ever welcome
Pelts down.
Hailstones like
Schoolyard marbles
Bounce and sizzle

Drenched
Like rats
Owen's words echo
In my ears

I'd rather finish off
With Paterson
Necessary
And important though
Owen's words
Are.

I'm not at all
In the mood
For words
Or thoughts of war

Patriotic

Yesterday I became a vegetarian
Signed the pledge
But market prices rose due to
Drought and working costs

When it was announced that
The country was plagued by the
Rabbit population
Patriotism for my country
Took a hold on me

I read the road signs
Eat a rabbit a day
Keep warm in a
Rabbit-skin coat

Put logic into practice
Smiled,
Gave up the pledge
And did my bit for my country.

Wild Things 2

You could take me where the wild things are
Let me see the other side of life
What a smorgasbord of experience
Would await me.

I'd see the brumbies running in the wind
Freedom all around them
Making their own rules
In their determined way

Their wild eyes flashing
Tomorrow will always have
To wait for them
In their untamed scheme of things.

Not My Desire

It is not my desire
As I sit by the fire
To own two pairs of
Crocodile shoes

I do not like the mammal
I'd rather the camel
If it came to the fact
I should chose

I once knew a girl
In a camel-hair coat
But she swore to the heavens
It came from the goat

Her reason for that
Is quite strange it is true
And last year that girl had
That coat dyed dark blue

Some people wear coats
Made from fur from the rabbit
And I think that's smart
Don't you think?

My friend, who is poor,
She's the woman next door
Tells all who may ask
Hers is mink.

The Question, the Answer

You ask, 'Did man land upon the moon?'
I think about it.
'Yes,' I say.
'Johnny Faulty's father says it's not true.'

I think some more.
'That's his opinion then.'

'Is he wrong?' my young child asks,
'Mum, is he wrong?'

I think about the nursery rhyme
I sang to him all those years ago,
The one about the cat and the fiddle
And the cow jumping over the moon.

My child tells me,
'That was all wrong, wasn't it?'
'It was a nursery rhyme,'
I tell him.

'Johnny Faulty's father
Says so was the man
Landing on the
Moon.'

Cicero

We quote Cicero

‘They do more harm
By their evil example
Than by their actual sin’

We applaud him

Our lives get busy
We forget him

It is when we look back
On history
We requote him
Applaud him

Wish we’d taken
More notice

What Cicero wrote
Was well worth the quote.

Blowflies

If you can bet on two flies
Climbing up a wall
It seems to me that you can
Bet on anything at all

How important is the blowfly
That he can gather fame
By being first to climb a wall
In a betting game.

Of course it's just a saying
To describe how much we bet
And I've yet to meet a winner
In my social set

I think the blowfly's ugly
He spreads germs, disease and stuff
And to bet on one is crazy,
It has to stop. Enough!

Just Like Dreyfus

I stand
Like a tree
Late autumn
Bereft of all leaves

I shiver
On a late
Winter's night
Unable to sleep

'Build a bridge
And get over it'
'Water off a duck's back'
'They probably didn't mean it'

Words, words, words,
Ad infinitum
Injustice is
Injustice

Dreyfus was cleared
In the end.
I can't wait
That long.

Looking For Ya

I looked for 'ya'
In the dictionary
('ya' as in
'See ya later')

Four-letter words
Are there for sure
I don't mean 'less'
I don't mean 'more'

But 'ya'
It hasn't reached the grade
It seems it's
Hidden in the shade

It's not a word
You'd find attractive
Even though
It's very active

'See ya later'
You will hear
Said five thousand
Times a year

The dictionary
Will just ignore it
It seems there's
Nothing going for it.

Jennifer's Auntie

Jennifer's auntie
Had us in stitches
She told us it was unlucky
To be superstitious

She told us all this
While washing the dishes
She told us to make sure
That we got all our wishes

And saved them
And kept them
And locked them away
Then good luck would
Stay with us
Day after day.

Just For the Record

We are here in the car
Held up on a major highway
Bumper to bumper
A weather change on the way
Distant thunder
Lightning flashes.

Could be here for hours
No sign of shops or service
The neighbour's mandarins in a bag
And a short supply of tonic water
All the time in the world
But little patience.

And patience is the
Curse of modern man
If we need more to moan about
All those pips in the mandarins
Will do it. You could spit chips.

The Dustman

The dustman, he was handsome
as mostly dustmen are
He calls each week by tractor
Most dustmen come by car.

We live up in the mountains
somewhere near boggy creek
This incident I write of
happened just last week

This time we didn't see him
Our dustbin courted flies
The sun shone hot
The creek ran dry
Some people lost their cool,
We can't live without the dustman
said one mad frustrated fool

They should sack him
when they find him
he's not worth a pinch of salt
But kind old Mrs Hennessy said
'Perhaps it's not his fault'

'That's exactly what she would say'
said her neighbour Mrs Flynn
'That woman is a whinger
I've never seen her grin'

No one knew the dustman's name
or even where he dwelt
The only information came
from someone who had said he smelt

Rumours now were running furious
everybody very curious
I think he's married to Patrice
You know, the vicar's lovely niece

'Oh no' said Abigail Mcquarter
'He married Mrs Porter's daughter'
That's wishful thinking
But he orta
I always thought he was a flirt
From what I hear now that's a cert

Well, at last the drought has broken
The dustman has been found
His tractor toppled over
He was pinned down to the ground

Poor fellow, he had shouted HELP
until his throat ran dry
It's a surety, he told himself,
That I am going to die

But fate, as fate does, intervened
Somebody smelled a rat
The flies around the tractor
were large, well fed and fat

In a tale that's told too often
of someone going missing
there is rumour, speculation
In the background someone hissing

There's a certainty
that someone there
knows something
they're not telling

And in cases such as rubbish tips
there's always something smelling
It's a fact of life
as someone says
and soon there'll be a find
a hint, a nudge, or something
of that kind

The dustman's now a hero
Magazines have contracts given
'You never know your fate' says he
'no matter wot's your livin'

Now the dustman's wealthy
It's acknowledged that he's healthy
He's invited out to dinner with the best
If you are asked one night to dine
to partake of the finest wine
your host could be the dustman of the year
Forget about your snobbery
when you go out hob nobbery
The laughter's on the other foot I hear.

www.ingramcontent.com/pod-product-compliance
Lightning Source LLC
Chambersburg PA
CBHW070102120526
44589CB00033B/1532
9781760414818